BRAZIL

TEXT: **M. WIESENTHAL**

1st. Edition, September 1978
I.S.B.N.
84-7424-054-9

Library of Congress Catalog Card Number: 78-63025
All rights reserved.
This edition is published by Crescent Books, a division of
Crown Publishers, Inc.

a b c d e f g h

CRESCENT BOOKS
New York

BRASILIA

On April 21, 1960, Brazil, a land full of magic, performed its most amazing trick when from the vast plains of the Central plateau it brought forth a whole brand-new city, matchless in its beauty. This feat took three years to accomplish.
It all started when on April 20, 1956, President Juscelino Kubitschek, giving form to the dream of the Brazilian Republic's First Constitution of erecting a new federal capital, sent Congress the so-called ''Message of Anapolis.'' This was approved by the Legislature and Senate in September of the same year, thus providing the town planner Lucio Costa and the architect Oscar Niemeyer with the funds to make possible that —so far— unequalled wonder called Brasilia.
Lucio Costa, the designer of Brasilia, gave it the shape of a large bird with open wings in the form of a cross. This symbolic design is at the same time functional. He gave a circulatory function to the curved axis, formed by the wings of this great bird of the future. The bird's outspread wings are

Bus Terminal. In the background the Praça dos 3 Poderes
(Three Powers square) - Brasília

Alvorada Palace.

Planalto Palace.

Praça dos 3 Poderes.

Another view of the Praça dos 3 Poderes.

high-speed arteries that meet smaller side-avenues distributing the local traffic, guiding it to the residential zones where Brasilia's visitors and residents live.

The body of this huge bird, or the staff of this large cross which is Brasilia, is mainly occupied by official centers. This is the monumental Brasilia, the Brasilia of Oscar Niemeyer, the architect of this unique capital. This is the Brasilia of the Palace of Alvorada, famous by its slight and elegant colonnades, the Palace of Planalto, the Palace of Itamaraty, the National Congress Hall, and so many other architectural masterpieces. It has been said: "These constructions were planned with some formal liberalism in mind and with an unlimited trust in the creative posibilities of Brazilian architecture."

But Brasilia is far more than a gigantic cross or a huge bird of cement, for Brasilia —a city in the likeness of the symbol of faith— is a fresh breeze from the future. Here the tourist can find what no other city can possibly offer him. Not even in Brazil. More than its buildings, more than the layout of these avenues through which circulates a population

Palace of Itamarati.

The Federal District Historical Museum.

The Federal District Historical Museum.

Supreme Federal Court.

AO PRESIDENTE JUSCELINO KUBITSCHEK DE
OLIVEIRA, QUE DESBRAVOU O SERTÃO E ERGUEU
BRASÍLIA COM AUDÁCIA, ENERGIA E CONFIANÇA. A
HOMENAGEM DOS PIONEIROS QUE O AJUDARAM
NA GRANDE AVENTURA.

Cathedral. Dome of the Cathedral.

Patron Saint of Brazil.

North Shopping Center. South Shopping Center.

South Shopping Center. South Financial Center.

whose latest census amounted to 1 million, it impresses, above all, by the feeling it gives of travelling in time, and leaving behind thousands of years of painful search, to enter a future —now a present— of hope, in a city made for and by man, remembering that man can not live where nature has been killed. And though it may be that Brasilia is all "head, body and wheels," and that it is impossible to live there without a vehicle, it is equally true that in Brasilia natural spaces compensate for cement, and that if the Ministry of Justice is a famous monument, so is the vast space of land occupied by the National Park. The recreational center of the city is not the fancy nightmarish lucubration of some great comtemporary architect; it is simply a copy of an older design, never paralleled, by that architect who created the world and provided us with earth and water, birds and fish. This recreational center is in fact, the lake of Paranoa, to which the designers of Brasilia cleverly added a complex of expensive restaurants where the tourist may try the tasteful dishes of the São Paulo "Bandeirantes" and emigrants from the North, accompanied by the most exotic fruit drinks.

Brasilia Bus Terminal.

One of Brasilias' huge city blocks.

Another view of the Bus Terminal.

Boarding ramps at the Bus Terminal.

Brasilia Airport.

Lake Paranoá.

Frequent flights link Brasilia to the rest of the country.

Downtown Porto Alegre.

PORTO ALEGRE

The descendants of the Azores islanders who came to the state of Rio Grande do Sul —then called the land of São Pedro— had to resist the fierce attacks of several invasions, frequently in the form of cavalry charges. Strengthened by these long sieges, the Italian and German emigrants, with their innate spirit of perseverance, gave birth to a new kind of people: the "gauchos," who still live on the southern borders of the country and are known for their love of an independent life-style.

The residents of Rio Grande do Sul live in the valley plantations, where they can harvest their crops of wheat, tobacco and grapes; and the tougher ones occupy the prairie lands, awaiting the coming of spring, when it is time to gather in millions of heads of cattle to brand them, and count the calves.

These two kinds of people meet in Porto Alegre (Happy Port), capital of the state, to celebrate their noisy "zafras" and cowboy parties.

This is why Porto Alegre with its more than a million people, bears this name; it is a city as happy, noisy and welcoming as its gauchos.

You do not need a professional guide to tour this city. In Porto Alegre every inhabitant is a willing guide, who will lead you to one of the lively "Casa de Chops" (typical beer-bars), or to the best place to enjoy a sea-food delicacy or a churrasco. You will always find an open house and welcoming people to share a casual, friendly chat. This is really true, for writers and most famous artists in the south of the country always keep the doors of their houses open, ready at any moment to greet friends and foreigners, if it possible for someone to be called a foreigner in Porto Alegre.

Boredom has been exiled from Porto Alegre, so there is no need to direct the visitor to any particular monument or entertainment. Just let yourself go, and sooner or later you will find yourself admiring a sunset on the Guaiba river; or tasting the traditional churrasco, accompanied by drinks made by delicious infusions of herbs. Maybe you will be sun-bathing on the riverside beaches or cheering one of the teams at the Beira-Rio stadium; unless you prefer to taste the thrills of a Formula 1 race at the Taruma raceway.

FLORIANOPOLIS

Located between Paraná and Rio Grande do Sul (Big river of the south) the state of Santa Catarina covers an area of almost 60.000 square miles, reaching from the Atlantic coast to the banks of the Uruguay river.

Monument to Júlio de Castilhos.

Porto Alegre -
The Cathedral.

Praça de
Matriz - Porto
Alegre.

Borges de Madeiros Avenue in downtown Porto Alegre. Legislative Assembly Hall. João Pessoa Avenue. Draw bridge. Stone bridge.

Araujo Viana Auditorium.

Lake in the Farroupilha Park.

A corner of the Farroupilha Park.

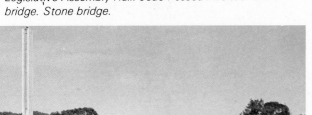

Santa Catarina well deserves the epithet of the most picturesque state of Brazil. It is a mosaic of ethnic groups living in a specific region. This, plus the beauty and variety of the geography —ranging from the sun-kissed beaches to the snows of São Joaquim, unique in Brazil— have made this state one of the tourist's favorite haunts.

In the midst of the attractive landscape of Santa Catarina. its capital Florianopolis stands out. This is a city with more than 150.000 inhabitants, and though the larger part is concentrated on an island, in fact it extends well beyond the island's western boundary mainland, and has taken over a portion of the shoreline called the Estreito (the Strait). Florianópolis is a well communicated city, with good hotels and sheltered beaches. Across the pages of its ancient buildings we can read the dynamic history of the island, with many chapters of piracy and wars of conquest waged by the Spanish and Portuguese.

With those days of conquest and piracy now far distant, Florianopolis today has become one of the most selected resorts for those who seek the tranquillity of the ocean. The island has a string of beaches where one can choose from the soft and gentle waves of the western shore, to the violent waters of the eastern region which is open to the ocean brakers.

And here on these beaches, Florianópolis offers the chance to discover one of the oldest traditions of Santa Catarina: the ''encajeras,'' women of skilful hands who twist a thread into intricate filigree work, keeping alive a tradition that goes back to the first Portuguese settlers who arrived from the Azores.

General view of Florianópolis.

On the same sandy beaches the tourist can visit old colonial forts, relics from those times when they were needed for defence against pirates and conquerors.

And while the waters in Florianópolis are warm and deliciously inviting, no less delicious are its shrimps, to be tasted in every restaurant, being beyond any doubt, the best sea-food in the country.

There are also interesting excursions to enjoy while in Florianopolis. Going towards the interior, but not too distant, can be found the old German colonies, specially in the green valley formed by the Atajai river, sometimes known as the "Brazilian Rhine."

If you prefer snow in a tropical sunny country, distant only 110 miles is the small but inviting city of São Joaquim.

CURITIBA

Capital of the state of Paraná, Curitiba exemplifies European colonization. This is a city with quiet streets and modern buildings, the latter limited to the city center, where the first Norman-style houses were built.

It is said that Curitiba was built from the top downwards. This is due to the custom that the European settlers had of building their homes on the hill-tops, up on the 2,700 feet heights, where the air is crystal clear. Later, new tides of emigrants, lured by the riches of Paraná, started to move to the slopes of the hills and enlarged —with an architecture of wide, open spaces —this city that

The Pink Palace.

Avenue of Arruda Ramos - Bahia Nova.

Public Market at Florianópolis.

15th of November Square.

Bahia Nova (New Bay) - Florianópolis.

Blumenau Street.

Monument to Hercílio Luz.

Aerial view of Curitiba.

Mural by Poty depicting the economic cycles of Paraná.

Another view of downtown Curitiba.

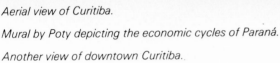

19th of December Square.

15th of November Street.

today has more than half a million residents.
To visit Curitiba is an experience, for this is a city where two ethnic groups meet and attempt to unite. During carnival time, blond dancers try to emulate the acrobatic steps and sorrowful rhythm of the black dancers of African ancestry. During the winter, old Slavs pace the streets in thick fur-coats and wearing headgear seemingly inherited from their forefathers, back on the frozen Central European steppes. This Saxon background of the greater part of Curitiba's people explains the strange fascination of a Brazilian city with tipically German food. Curitiba is the starting point of a tour that is a must for any traveler: Vila Velha. After 40 miles of roads, one arrives at a ruined city of crumbling rock, walls, and uncovered excavations. This is a fascinating

city, curiously sculpted by the wind, that over long periods of time has carved out phantasmagoric monuments out of the stone, using fine grains of sand as its only chisel.
A little further away —but nevertheless reachable— are the beaches of Paraná. A train-ride from Curitiba to the port of Parangua will not be regretted, for the visitor can enjoy through the windows of his train a truly magnificent panorama.

FOZ DE IGUAÇU
Further away, about 300 miles from Curitiba, is the mouth of the river Iguaçu (Foz de Iguaçu), where the majestic sight of water falling 240 feet, between walls of rugged stone, impresses the visitor.

Santos Andrade Square.

Another view of Curitiba.

*Generoso
Marques
Square.*

Vila Velha (The Old Ville) - Paraná.

Another panorama of Vila Velha.

Rock formations in Vila Velha.

Saint Martin Hotel - Iguaçu.

Façade of the Hotel das Cataratas. (Waterfalls' Hotel).

General view of the same hotel.

This is the wild thunderous beauty of a Brazil still primitive, which at the river Iguaçu delights our eyes with places of incomparable beauty.

The mouth of the river is half-hidden in the thickets of a natural park that also demarks tha border of Brazil with Argentine and Paraguay. The visitor, welcomed by comfortable hotel and transportation facilities, is led through this park of wild splendor, which, suddenly opens out into an even more striking scene: the magnificent waterfall, formed by a semicircular curtain of fine jets, that hit the bottom with a deafening roar. The tourist can walk down by the narrowest of pathways, carved out of the rocks, right to the bottom of the huge cascades, and from there gaze at the constant rainbow of a sun shaded by gauzes of mist.

Further up, the Iguaçu river offers us the beauty of its crooked course, over uneven ground, sometimes cutting down deeper than 280 feet. This is a mighty river, 2 miles wide, splashing and tumbling in watery thunder. Automatic elevators and protective ropes make it easy to watch this amazing natural show, seldom presented by nature.

SÃO PAULO

In the year of 1533, the Jesuits José de Anchieta and Manoel de Nobrega, founded a small cathechist school for the indians somewhere in the high plains, between the rivers Anhaugabao and Tamanduatei. That school is today a city of eight million people, capital of the state bearing the same name.

Viewing stand over the Iguaçu Falls.   *General view of the Iguaçu Falls.*

The scene in Iguaçu is ever changing.

A different view of the Iguaçu Falls

One of the most beautiful of the falls.

Brazil-Paraguay International Bridge.

Hotel Saint Martin - Pool.

Praça da Sé.

Monument to Anchieta.

*Ibirapuera Park. Monument to the heroes of the
revolution of '32.*

Detail of the monument to the founders of Sâo Paulo.

Ibirapuera. Monument of the Flags.

Monument to Independence.

Chá Viaduct.

Saint Anthony's church.

Monastery of São Bento.

São Paulo is not only one of the highly populated cities in the world, but also one of the most beautiful. It is a cement and asphalt monster, where the visitor stands in awe, overwhelmed by the beauty of the artificial. As has often been remarked, if Rio de Janeiro is natural beauty, divine beauty, São Paulo is man-made beauty, the artificial beauty of the daring hand of man. Everything in São Paulo is an aberration created by human delirium, even its average of 6.000 people per square mile in a country of huge empty spaces. In Sao Paulo everything is absurd, everything is intoxicating, almost terrifying. This city is a once-in-a-lifetime experience, like a pathological attraction, a tropical frenzy. That is why São Paulo is like Rio; in order to know it you have to visit it. All we can say is that this human delirium

Cathedral of São Paulo.

Side view of the Cathedral.

Cathedral of São Paulo-Door.

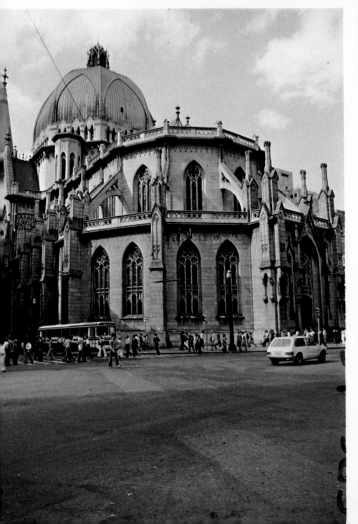

Entrance lobby of the Municipal Theater.

The Stage room of the Municipal Theater.

Municipal Theater of São Paulo.

Panoramic view of downtown
São Paulo.

Roosevelt Square.

Paulista Avenue.

Valley of Anhangabaú.

Interior of the Municipal
Theater.

Paulista Museum.

Valley of Anhangabaú by night.

made city, this dream of some crazy genius turned into reality, besides being this, a frentic mirage, boasts a planetarium which is unique in the world, and superb museums where you can see masterpieces of human genius, zoos filled with amazing fauna, churches of striking beauty, such as the Metropolitan Cathedral, parks where products of human inventiveness are in constant exhibition, natural forests, like the forest of Morumbi, reservoirs with beaches where water sports can be practiced, a beautiful ocean close by the city, and a wild night-life with all kinds of shows and entertainment, plus a Chinatown, exotic restaurants, and...
São Paulo is a populous metropolis, colorful and

Praça da Republica (Square of the Republic) by night.

alive, where man has set his craziness and his sanctity. São Paulo is a wine that has to be tasted.

RIO DE JANEIRO

What can be said about Rio that has not already been said? The densely populated capital of the state of Guanabara —until 1960 capital of Brazil— is perhaps the most written-about metropolis in the whole world. Millions of words have been printed to try to express it, but the truth is that those millions of words are no more than a collection of dead "cliches." None of these expressions is Rio, for Rio de Janeiro cannot be described in words. Rio

Museum of Modern Art.

Race-track at Cidade Jardim (Garden City).

The Japanese district of São Paulo.

Pacaembu Stadium.

Municipal Library.

Bus Terminal - São Paulo.

Another view of the Bus Terminal.

Congonhas Airport.

Detail of the Arts & Crafts Fair at the Praça da Republica.

The tourist always finds a large variety of typical Brazilian stones at the Fair.

Diverse objects for sale at the Arts & Crafts Fair.

Brazilian folklore on show at the Arts & Crafts Fair.

Many visitors come to the Arts & Crafts Fair.

Sâo Paulo's Zoo.

Reptiles at the Zoo.

Ibirapuera Park - Planetarium.

Another view of the Ibirapuera Park.

The wild animals run free at the Simba Safari.

Guarujá - São Paulo.

The parakeet vendor, a local character in Santos.

Panoramic view of the beaches of Santos.

is a city to be lived, not told about. If you want to know what Rio is, just dive into it, live it, become one with Rio and let it become you. Afterwards, when you return home tired but satisfied, from this incomparable adventure, all you can do is store it in your memory as the most precious of your souvenirs. If someone, knowing that you have been to Rio, asks you what it is like, all you will be able to say is that Rio is just... Rio. What else could you say? Is it any good to explain that Rio is jet-black nigths, psychedelic "macumbas," a magical carnival, wild sambas, or maybe the peace and quiet of its beaches, the surprises of its museums, the tranquillity of its parks, the thrills of a foot-ball match at the Maracaná, the miracle of Paquetá, and among many other wonders, the warm embrace of the Corcovado? No. These are just rusty words. Rio is... Rio.

SAMBA

Deprive Brazil of music and you will see it die. Because Brazil is music. The Brazilian feeds on music and sweats music. For a Brazilian, life is not life if it can not be sung, not with the long, sorrowful

Pão de Azucar

*The Renowned Carnival of Rio.
Samba Schools' Parade.*

Ipanema Beach

steps of a tango, but with short spasmodic movements to the rhythm of a samba, marked by slight beats of the "maracas."

The word samba, of African origin, has a double meaning. It can be translated as "melancholy" or as "belly music." And this is what the samba basically is: The melancholy, drawn out from the body by a rhythm that is happy, playful and full of promises, marked by sensual navel movements of a belly replete with life.

When today you say Brazil you say samba, but it was not so at the beginning of this century, when the samba was not yet Brazil. Then the samba was the Brazil of the black people only, and belonged to them. But that first black samba of spasmodic cadencies, candomble trances and the misery of "favela" life, has today become the rhythm of a country, a standard of tight skin and warm promises symbolizing the vital power of an extraordinary country.

THE CARNIVAL

Every year for four days, the people of Rio de Janeiro forget how to sleep. All, absolutely all the residents of the city, synchronize their muscles and flex them

to the same rhythm, the rhythm of the "batucada" (samba orchestras).

But the Carnival is more than just dancing, for it is a wild party where each inhabitant of Rio, —as well as of other cities in Brazil, for the Carnival does not belong solely to Rio— makes his dreams come true. "During Carnival time" —say Brazilians— "each and every one of us lives his own phantasy". So, women dress up or undress, and more or less dressed, most of them live in a fantastic realm taken from the Arabian nights. Men also play at trying to make their fantasies reality. The Carnival is the great festival of the transvestite. The mulatto girls of elastic legs and warm bellies fill the air with the sensual poetry of their orgiastic convulsive dances. This is life saturating the streets, a life of uninhibited movement, that in the most perfect of psychodramas, liberates all tensions and sorrows... and the morning after, a new day dawns, clean, fresh, and shining, to give life once again to a happy, welcoming Brazil full of promises and surprises, betwitching its tourists, whose clouds just vanish into the sunny sky of Brazil.

BELO HORIZONTE

This is a populous city, with more than a million

Rio Branco Square - Belo Horizonte

Amazon Avenue.

7th of September Square.

Rui Barbosa Square.

inhabitants. Belo Horizonte was thoroughly planned before it was built, for it was supposed to take the place of Ouro Preto as the capital of the wealthy mountain state of Minas Gerais. Ten years after its conception, Belo Horizonte was born in the year of 1897.

Although Belo Horizonte is a modern city, with stark outlines, the city does not lack the urban attractions of a metropolis. Whoever walks its streets will surely find a harmonious display of fine buildings, among which he will admire the Art Museum, the Casa de Baile (the Dancing House), the Yatch Club, the Chapel of Saõ Francisco, decorated by the artist Candido Portinari, and the Palacio de la Libertad, seat of the state Governor, situated in the middle of a park adorned with regal palm trees and blooming rosebushes. We must also mention the reservoir of Pampulha, the great lake which was model for Brasilia's artificial one.

But of course Belo Horizonte is not merely an assortment of monuments. This is above all a living city, with luxury hotels, gay night-clubs and memorable restaurants where the local "minera"

food can be savored. Belo Horizonte is a brilliant city, whose warm nights can never be forgotten.
In the same state of Minas Gerais the tourist will visit the historic city of Ouro Preto, formerly the state capital and today preserved as a monument.
In Ouro Preto the oldest civil buildings remain intact; they are two-story houses whose balconies have lathe-crafted wooden banisters. This is an enchanted citty dotted with valuable eighteenth and early nineteenth century temples, and typical "Pasos" —tiny chapels where, during Holy Week processions comparable only to those held in Seville, Spain, the "penitentes," stepping forward, stop to rest and pray from time to time.
To sum up, Ouro Preto is a live monument to the history of Minas Gerais.

SALVADOR
Founded in 1549 on the top of a hill, Salvador is today the capital of the state of Bahia, and until 1763 was the capital of Brazil. This is a city that grew

General view of Ouro Preto

Church of São Francisco de Paula.

Chapel of N.S. das Merces. (Our Lady of the Mercy).

Pilar Church.

Praça Tiradentes in Ouro Preto.

Mining school in Ouro Preto.

Rua Direita (Straight street) - Ouro Preto.

Lacerda elevator.

Sculpture by Mario Cravo.

Beach at the Porto da Barra.

Santa Maria Fort.

Beach at the Farol da Barra.

and grew always expanding downwards towards the majestic ocean of the Bay of Todos los Santos, (All Saints Bay).

Salvador, old city of jutting roofs, displays to the visitor the many stages of its development. About this city it has been said: "Majestic churches, whose roofs are platted with skilfully worked gold, in a town of narrow streets and steep stairways winding down the mountain-side; ancient courtyards and stern fortresses, hiding deeds and old legends behind their impressive stone façades. Everywhere traces are visible of the old political and cultural capital of colonial times; but the symmetry of the baroque architecture is broken by the modern-day buildings with their aggressive lines. These new monuments, together with the tunnels, viaducts and raised walkways, are a testimony of the development of the modern Salvador, an active regional center with more than a million inhabitants."

This is Salvador, a city where the hectic life of its industrial and commercial activities goes hand in hand with the quiet "Ladeira de Pelourinho," one of the most beautiful examples of colonial architecture, and a shoreline of strikingly beautiful beaches where Salvador finds rest. Its sanctuaries have been made into museums of the past: The Museum of Sacred Art, housing sculptures, paintings, silverware and panels from the sixteenth century; the Museum of Carmo, with valuable statues, oratories and varied sacred objects, and the Museum of Recôncavo, portraying the economic and social life of this region over a period of three centuries.

Salvador is indeed one of the largest tourist centers, displaying a continuous contrast between the old and the modern. Thus, we can find a replica of sports played today in the "capoeira," a wrestling contest transformed by the black people into a war-dance;

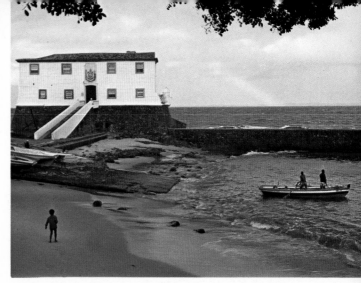

Church of "Senhor do Bonfim". Souvenirs for sale.
Woman selling regional dishes. Souvenirs and
balangandas. Church of São Francisco.

Farol da Barra. (Lighthouse of Barra).

Young people of Bahia on the beach at Porto da Barra.

and even the Catholic religion has a unique expression in Salvador, with 165 gold plated churches in Ciudad Alta (the upper city), where the Catholic saints stand side by side with the "orixás" (gods). To the sorrowful religious canticles of the "novenas," Salvador has added the deep sound of the pagan "atabaques." The same phenomenom is observed in the kitchen: modern cuisine and delicious African dishes are served together, creating delicacies that no visitor should ignore, for instance "vatapá" (shrimps and fish stewed in coconut milk), "saravá" (black beans with small shrimps), "xinxim" (chicken with dry shrimps), "carurú" (tongue with shrimps and onions) and the "sarapatel" (a dish of pork cooked in lemon juice). Salvador is a city where yesterday and today become one to form a uniquely attractive scene.

ARACAJU

Aracaju, with more than 200.000 inhabitants, is the capital of the state of Sergipe. This is a state of

General view of Aracajú.

13.000 square miles, situated on the seashore north of Bahia, and specially famous for the fierce battles the French fought against the indomitable Portuguese settlers four centuries ago.

This small state, with its pleasant climate and interesting history, had its first capital in the baroque city of Saõ Cristobal, until 1885 when Aracaju became the state's center.

Aracaju is a modern city built only 100 years ago. Thus, its architecture is geometrical and lineal. Its streets and avenues meet at right angles starting from the central core, at either side of the Sergipe river. It is said that in Aracaju it is always easy to find the ocean. And this is true, for the ocean is indeed at the end of every street. So it is hardly worth mentioning that while in Aracaju, the tourist must seek out its betwitching ocean beaches, where at sunset the sea breeze plays in the tops of the "cajueiro" trees, laden with yellow and red fruits. The "cajueiros" form the natural decoration of the dunes of Aracaju, some semi-desert and others crowded with Brazilian food restaurants. But everywhere one can enjoy the peace and rest pervading this gentle and civilized corner of nature. Ocean bathing in a pleasant climate, short boat tours to nearby beaches, typical dishes accompanied by sweet music... this is Aracaju. And on the way back to the hotel, in front of the port, stands the Modelo Market, where there is a varied and characteristic display of clay and straw objects. These simple crafted souvenirs will remind us —when on our return home— of quiet Aracaju, a city whose simplicity won our hearts.

RECIFE

On the delta of the Papibaribe river, sheltered by promontories and islands, stands Recife, the capital of the state of Pernambuco, which with a population of more than 1.200.000 inhabitants, is the largest urban center in the northeast of Brazil.

Monument to General Voladao.

Fausto Cardoso Park - Aracajú.

Church of Our Lady of Carmo - Recife.

Recife grew up from a fishing colony and its name Recife (reef) comes from the stretch of reefs protecting the port. Of the old Recife founded by the Dutch in 1630 nothing remains today. The Recife of today is a modern, industrialized city, with thousands of vehicles circulating through its avenues; it is always on the go due to the constant movement of varied merchandise, specially intense in the port, which is a modern one, perfectly equipped for the rapid dispatch of sugar, the state's main source of wealth.

But the crystalline beauty of Recife's beaches is not

Boavista Park - Recife.

Downtown Recife.

Church of Our Lady da Penha.

Beach of the Boa Viagem (Pleasant journey).

affected by the big city bustle, and remain the greatest attraction for visitors; quiet beaches, with almost still water like ocean lagoons, thanks to the protection afforded by the reefs; white sandy beaches dotted with swaying coconut-palms that shade the small beer-bars where relaxing conversation continues well into the small hours of the night.

However, Recife the "Brazilian Venice" is not only famed for its wonderful beaches, for it also has a large number of historical monuments dating from Dutch colonial times, and many magnificent churches preserving costly relics left behind by the Portuguese colonists. Also notable are the Museo del Açucar (the Sugar Museum) and the Anthropology Museum of the Joaquim Nabudo Institute, which owns the largest collection of votive-offerings in the country.

On the other hand, Recife has been able to keep alive its purest cultural traditions, so the visitor can enjoy a varied repertoire of folk dances including the "bumba-mei-boi" that portrays the life and death of an ox, as well as the "maracatu," a carnival-like parade, dating from times of slavery, with colored "kings" and lively minstrelsy.

Recife is also the capital of the clay and ceramic sculptors. This is something the traveler must keep in mind when gathering souvenirs in a city that besides its unique beaches has many other things to offer.

NATAL

With almost 400.000 residents, Natal is the capital of the state of Rio Grande do Norte (Big river of the North), economically sustained by its fishing industry, mainly based on the lobster. Natal is,

View of the Fort of the Reis Magos (the Three Wise Men).

General view of Natal.

Cannon at the Fort of the Reis Magos.

A different view of the Fort of the ''Reis Magos''.

Monument to Independence.

therefore, a city-port, with several fishing colonies stretching along soft sandy beaches and enjoying an enviable temperature.

Natal was founded on December 25, 1599, at an ideal spot, where river, ocean and land meet in harmonious conjunction. This city, born under auspicious omens, is today a metropolis with luxurious hotels, exquisite restaurants and all kinds of entertainment.

Monument-wise, the greatest attraction in this city is the old fortress of the Reis Magos, built in the shape of a star long before the city was founded. Today this fortress houses the Museum of Popular Art.

At the base of the fortress, by the "saeteras," where the sixteenth century Portuguese bow-men replied to the attacks of French pirates, we find the main attraction of Natal: its beaches. The Forte beach, surrounded by reefs that form a natural, intimate pool; the beach of Areia Profeta, preferred by the young for its natural beauty that sets off the good looks of the bathers, who offer their skin, almost all of it, to the sun; and many other beaches, perhaps with fewer bronzed youngsters, but with no less scenic beauty.

There is no need even to comment on the regional food of this marine city which like Fortaleza, offers the best Atlantic sea-food obtainable, or to praise its "sisal" craftsmanship, nor even to sing the glories of the Bosque dos Namorados (Forest of Lovers) with its mild temperature, its lush vegetation and its gentle illumination; however, we feel something must be said about the "Ararunas," a folk-dance society which brings together groups of native fishermen and handcraftsmen, all of them eager to keep alive the dances loved by their ancestors. These are peasant dances, extremely interesting, with the male performers wearing a frock coat, white pants and a top hat. This is the magical Natal, sharing with us its ancestral fears in the rhythms of its dances.

FORTALEZA

Capital of the state of Ceara, Fortaleza is a city of 900.000 residents living at close quarters with the ocean. And the ocean is everything in Fortaleza, for all the state of Ceará, and Fortaleza itself, practically live off the ocean. As the dawn breaks, the "jangadas," those frail and rustic boats, comprised of wooden planks and a triangular sail —typical of Ceara— sail out to sea in search of

Alberto Maranhâo Theater - Natal.

Potengi River.

*Coconut palms
in Natal.*

*Views of
the beach in
Areia Preta.*

*Beach of Meio -
Natal.*

*Downtown
Mangue - Natal.*

Fishermen of Natal. Fishing boat. Northern raft.

Back from the ocean, the raftsmen sell the fish on the beach.

Raftsmen in Fortaleza.

shoals of fish and shell-fish reserves. The latter, after being frozen, are exported, this being the main source of wealth in the state.
Fortaleza was founded in 1695 around a Dutch fort, and today is a bright city of white houses and straight streets, the center bordering on the sea.

All life's activities are centered on the ocean; it is here down by the ocean that its products are traded, and here too, man finds solace in its wide beaches dotted with tiny family restaurants using recipes passed down by black slaves that turn the food into a dish fit for the gods. And indeed it is fit for the

Monument to Iracema.

Cearense Craftswork.

Water carrier.

gods, for these recipes were originally prepared to please the gods, who, after all, are also connoisseurs of good food.

It is said that the sea is the cradle of artists, and it must be so, for in the beer-bars on the white dunes of Fortaleza art is spoken as an everyday topic, creating an art that comes out onto the streets, a truly popular art. It is on the streets that the artists of the "primitive" school of Ceará display their works, propping the pictures up against the house fronts; these artists are considered to be the best in the country.

Womenfolk too, are artists in Fortaleza; all sailors' wives in Ceará, in the open shade of their balconies, untiringly twist the abstract and intricate patterns of the "bilro" (bone) laces, making delicate

decorative articles in pastel colors, that seem as if they were woven out of shells and foam, or out of the sand and the sun of Fortaleza.

BELEM

Belem, the capital of the state of Pará was founded in the small fort of the Presepio, built in 1616 by Francisco Caldeira. That little fort is today a city with more than 800.000 people; and what is more important for all the tourists who come here is that Belem is the door to the Amazon. This means that in Belem the traveler may experience the most excitement packed holiday schedule in a city where adventure is still possible. But Belem also offers,

70

Vista Mar District.

Cool green ocean waters.

Square in downtown Fortaleza.

Cathedral of Belém.

besides its typical attractions and primitive landscape all the comforts of modern life. The conjunction of nature with the artificial, and the blending of vegetation with modern conveniences is so succesful that it can be experienced and enjoyed in its streets and plazas, havens of lush greenery.

Its culture and picturesque fairs, its music of elemental rhythms, its amerindian flavored cuisine, its popular art and night-life, plus many other exciting facets, are all linked to the unique atmosphere that is Belem. Here it is always summer, a summer whose temperature averages 70° F. This is the Belem that welcomes you with the sweet

Giant trees - Belém.

Marajoara ceramics.

São Bias Market.

Ver-O-Peso Market.

Ramp at the Ver-O-Peso Market.

scents of virgin jungle and primeval woman; also it is the Belem of clear, and bright skies, where the beauty of this city-landscape is reflected and one does not know where the city begins or nature ends. A must for the tourist is a visit to the Old City with its large old houses and impressive tiled colonial façades. So is the Cathedral, the Museum of Sacred Art and so many other buildings of striking architectural beauty.

Other places that should not be missed are: the already mentioned fort of Presepio, from where one can enjoy the long Bay of Guajará; the La Paz Theater (Peace Theater; the Paraense Emilio Goeldi Museum, the only museum existing in Brazil dedicated to Amazon Anthropology; the Rodriguez

Alves Forest, with its Amazonian greenery; and the Crafts Fair.

Belem is also ocean and beaches, and for those who want to enjoy ocean delights, there is nothing better than a week-end on the island of Mosqueira, with its fluvial beaches and sea-food.

MANAUS

Built right in the midst of tropical jungle, Manaus is the capital of the state of Amazonas, with more than 300.000 people, and is passing today through a phase of rapid expansion that has caused its designation as a Free Tax Zone. Today this

Entrance to the Rodrigues Alves Forest.

View of the Rodrigues Alves Forest.

The forest displays a unique collection of tropical birds.

Turtles' Paradise.

inhospitable part of the country, once travelled at great risk to his life by Francisco de Orellana, has in Manaus one of the most modern air transportation facilities in South America. And what is most unusual and amazes the tourist in Manaus, is the sight of a people winning the fight against nature, building a most comfortable and even luxurious and sophisticated city in the heart of the jungle. Manaus today is already a cosmopolitan city, with elegant buildings, bright and well provided commercial centers, a lively flow of traffic, and five-star hotels and entertainment. In Manaus the jungle has been banished, although it can be experienced close by the city, to the delight of the tourist, who may enjoy the most sensational natural wonders on short guided tours, that in the evenings bring him back to the comfort of his hotel. You can participate in excursions down the river to Januarylandia, where, apart from sampling regional dishes in floating restaurants, you will also encounter dreamy lakes and navigate the dark waters of the Black river up to the place where it

Cathedral Square - Manaus.

Fine paving in the streets of Manaus.

Praça da Catedral (Cathedral Square) - Manaus.

Another view of the Cathedral.

Eduardo Ribeiro Avenue - Manaus.

River port - Manaus.

Amazon Theater.

Praça do Teatro (Theater Square) - Manaus.

Amazon Theater, architectural jewel of Manaus.

*Curtain of the Amazon
Theater. Below: Detail
of the boxes and galleries*

*Entrance lobby of the
Amazon Theater.*

meets the Solimões river. This excursion can only be compared to the one you can take overland, this time to Turislandia, where forests of singular beauty await your visit.

But the visit to Manaus is not over when you have seen its lakes and their beaches, not even after having done some fishing there, for Manaus is also a city: the Amazonas theater, of superb architecture; the Museum of the Indian, where life of the Amazonic indian is portrayed in all its aspects; the Zoo, with its large variety of Amazonic animals, even with some extinct species; also the shopping area. In the Free-Tax Zone you will find all kind of articles as well as the most beautiful objects of Indian craftsmanship. Manaus is also a happy city with a distinctive and very attractive carnival and a wealth of popular fiestas, and among many other things worth mentioning, its food, Brazilian and at the same time very varied, based on an abundance of fish fauna that is unique in the world, as are the many exotic fruits in the city, where everything is unique and unrepeatable, just as the Amazon river

Orchestra seats at the Amazon Theater.

Impressive ceiling of the Amazon Theater.

is also unique and unrepeatable.

A CONTINENT-WITHIN-A-COUNTRY

But Brazil is more, much more than its cities, Brazil is a country covering almost five million square miles, extending from Ecuador to the Tropic of Capricorn. It is, therefore, a real continent-within-a-country with a wide variety of geographical and human scenary. Landscapes ranging from the rocky heights of Piaui, to the still unexplored jungles of the Amazon river; and human landscapes varying from the primitive natives of the interior —with their almost magical culture to

Manaus Market.

Rio Negro (The Black River).

the descendants of the first Central European emigrants, originators of a technological culture. So, it is not strange that in Brazil, where the landscape is so heterogeneous, animal and vegetal is plentiful, and the human family diverse, there is also a wide kaleidoscope of popular expressions.

THE AMAZON

So, besides the sensual Brazil of the beaches, there is another Brazil, austere, almost ascetic, to be uncovered in the regions of the interior, as well as a primitive, almost asphyxtiating and exciting Brazil, the one belonging to that river-ocean called the Amazon.

The Amazon is the largest river basin in the world. The river which is 3,500 miles long (2,000 miles in Brazilian territories), discharges into the Atlantic Ocean —through a mouth more than 60 miles wide— almost 420.000 cubic feet of water per second.

This inmense natural wonder crosses the large

Detail of the Alto Araguaia (Mato Grosso).

The Trans-Amazonic Highway.

Palafita (Riverside house).

tertiary plain between the high plateau of the Guyanas and the Central Brazilian plain. This is a characteristic river of the plains, for when it enters Brazil its height is just 240 feet above sea level. This makes it navigable over its entire course, even for ocean liners.

It was the Spaniards, who, in 1538, first navigated the Amazon starting in Quito and following the course of the waters. And only a century later, the Portuguese explorer Pedro Texeira, accomplished the same feat, this time against the current, opening the way to the ships that during the eighteenth century sailed up and down the 12,000 fluvial miles of the Amazon and its tributaires.

The Amazon of today, besides being the great gateway to Brazil, also nurtures large cultivated areas and provides exciting adventure that no tourist with a spirit of conquest can forget. This is the adventure in which modern man, sunk in everyday city life, can find the genuine heart-beat of his existence. This emotion will take us back to a space and a time where man was wholly satisfied by his own recourses, still untouched by the ruthless mechanism of our civilization of pulleys and engines.

THE INDIANS

The indian tribes, spread over a great part of the country, mainly in the Amazon river basin, are just a minority of the total population of Brazil. In a country with almost 107 million people, the Brazilian indians scarcely number 80.000.

These natives, seemingly doomed to extinction, have recently shown a significant population increase, thanks to the dedication of a government agency, the FUNAI (a federal organization created for the protection of the indian), bringing the indians closer to civilization, teaching them new ways to improve their crops, as well as new manual work techniques. At present there are approximately 60,000 indians under the protection of the FUNAI, all of them living in large reserves, such as the park

In the Xingu Valley, a young Kalapalo indian grinding manioc.

. Youngman of the Yawalapiti tribe smoking his long cigar by the Xingu river shore.

of Xingú; in these centers thousands of indians learn new cultural skills, and more effective production techniques so that the future contact with a more developed society can happen more naturally and without trauma. But this is, undoubtedly, a difficult task. The indians possess their own culture, a millennarian culture that bears no similarity to our modern civilization, and they can hardly comprehend the need to leave behind their simple life so close to nature to become part of that other cement and steel life of the big cities.

IN THE WORLD OF MAGIC

Africa lives in Brazil. Through these pages we have met it in a cook-up of onomatopeia: "vatapá," "carurú," "acarajé," "moqueca," "xinxim," "cocada..." a blend of primeval tastes destined to feed the gods. The gods that seem to come to life in the thousands of grimaces, games and rites, which, as if they came from a magical world, strike

our amazed eyes even on the streets of the Brazilian cities. This is the magic of the intricate feet movements of the "capoeira", the karate which came from Angola, practiced by children in some streets of Bahia. It is a refined kind of karate, with blows and steps following the rhythm of the music. This is the musical algebra of the African soul, today's soul of a freed people searching for its identity in that calisthenics of a black samurai. White masks on black skins; in Brazil the African soul has not repudiated its divinities. "Oxum" is still the goddes of beauty, "Oxossi" guides the arm of the hunters, "Ogum" decides the result of wars, and "Oba" and "Yemanja" still rule over rivers and oceans. This is so, even though "Ogum" is now called Saint Anthony, "Oxumare," Saint Bartholomew and "Oxoss," Saint George. For these people, the "orixas," raised from the cemetery of African deities are still living under the skins of these Christian saints.

East Amazon indians, displaying multicolored necklaces.

A young indian.

Kamayura indian.

Karajá indian.

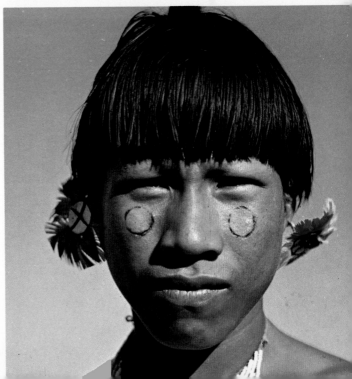

The "Candomble" rite.

And from this fusion and mixture of beliefs the "candomble" was born, that "voodoo" from Bahia that every evening stirs the air on the hills of Salvador.

The tam-tam are beaten tirelessly and no less untiringly the rounds of dancers, dressed up like monks, try to summon the saints ("orixás"). And the "orixás" come into the shuddering, sweating bodies of the dancers, who then fall down in a trance; and as they enter into this trance, in a hypnotic show for the tourists, their helpers come to dry off the sweat, saliva, etc... "This is the weird kingdom of Jean Rouch and his 'crazy teachers'," —wrote Charles Vanhecke— "the kingdom of black priests, like that queen of the candomble, Menininha de Gantois, whose real name is Maria Escolastica, who has more authority over the faithful than the archbishops of the 'praça de Se'."

Afro-Brazilian rites

Capoeira wrestlers.

This is the magical world of Brazil, the world of candomblé in Bahia, and of macumba and umbanda in Rio, these two latter rites similar to the first mentioned, except that these are strongly impregnated with black magic. This is also the world of a cuisine based on palm-oil and African flavors. A world of Carnival, and definitely belonging to a kind of people who seem to perspire music, with the rhythm of nature in their blood, because —fortunately— they still are part of nature, living close to the open air, to the water, the trees and the fire.

FAUNA AND FLORA

In such a large country as Brazil, it is understandable that its vegetation displays the widest possible range of varieties, numbering thousands, from the coarse plants of the seaside, to the Equatorial Amazon wildwoods. In Brazil one can find tropical, subtropical and Equatorial vegetation in all its varied harmonies to be admired in many parks, all open to the public. We will mention the Botanical Garden, with its mission of enhancing children's love of nature, the National Park of Itatiaia, of vivid scenery, the National Park of La Sierra de los Organos, set between the cities of Petropolis and Teresopolis, with its granite heights, the National Park of Iguaçu, with its sparkling waterfalls, the National Park of Paulo Alfonso, beside the San Francisco river which also has several cascades, the National Park of the Grotto of Ubajará, in the state of Ceará, housing the curious geological monument called "Gruta de Ubajara" (Grotto of Ubajara); and also the National Parks of "Bananal" and the "Amazon Valley," the former lies in the state of Goias and the latter between the rivers Xingu and Tocantis, tributaries of the Amazon. We should not forget that when travelling by the Amazon river we are in close contact with the Equatorial plant life in all its natural and luxuriant beauty; that unique vegetable world where trees of thickly-closed tops form the base where other trees take root, these in turn supporting a third layer of trees, forming the so-called "cathedral-forests," with its three floors of vegetation. These are enclosed forests, with lianas and roots entangled in a web where life is constantly simmering its powerful splendor. The animal life too, for the Amazonic fauna is of superlative interest to all visitors to the Brazilian National Parks, having a variety of jaguars, pumas and wildcats, alligators and piranhas, and what is worst, the ants, spiders and anopheles, the little insects being paradoxically

the most dangerous of all living creatures in the Equatorial area.

"The small expedition," —wrote Sir Conan Doyle— in his book 'A Lost World,' writing about the Amazonic flora and fauna- "had to face at every turn of the path all the dangers and difficulties peculiar to the virgin jungle. A thick tangle of a dozen different varieties of trees blocked their way, and the green trunks were hidden by lianas, ivy and all sorts of climbing plants. The explorers stumbled continuosly over poisonous plants, often displaying huge flowers of different colors: crimson, pink, yellow, and most frequently orange, while on the wild herbage all sorts of reptiles and insects crawled and crept: gigantic venomous serpents, boas, deadly insects and spiders whose bite drives people mad. This was a region where man had to be constantly on the alert."

"Bumba Meu Boi" - Maranhao.

INDEX

Printed in Spain GEOCOLOR®